DRIED
FLOWER
IDEAS

DRIED FLOWER IDEAS

Rosemie Strobel-Schulze

CHANCELLOR
PRESS

Contents

This book is dedicated to my mother,
and through her to all mothers.
I am grateful for her love, which has time and again
helped me in all life's situations.

Introduction

The shepherds on thy pasture walks
The first fair cowslip finds
Whose tufted flowers on slender stalks
Keep nodding in the winds.

And tho thy thorns withhold the may
Their shades the violets bring
Which children stoop for in their play
As tokens of the spring.

There is an old saying that forget-me-nots never wilt, and indeed, with my method of drying, their beautiful colour now can remain bright and vibrant for a long time.

I used to believe that the best way of drying was simply to hang the plants up. Now I have found that preserving with silica gel is an even better method, and I would naturally like my readers to profit from my knowledge. However, I would like to do more than just explain the silica gel drying method to you. Following the yearly sequence of holidays and festivals, I want to bring back to life old customs, some of which have almost sunk into obscurity. I believe that most people like to have firm traditions to hold on to.

Many of us still eat the same sort of meals with the family on feastdays like Christmas, New Year and Easter that our mother gave us as children. And every year we may build a Christmas crib together, or make Easter decorations with our children and paint blown eggs to hang from them. These things are fun, strengthen family bonds and are a profitable and creative way to spend the family's free time.

First of all I would like to introduce you to my personal sort of recycling and recommend that you follow it. It is almost a fixation for me to try and find further use for things that are seemingly finished with, just rubbish. When you have a constructive hobby, all sorts of things come in handy. Most important, this is a way to show children what a lot of pretty things can be made at

very little expense by using imagination and creativity to transform the many different products of our surplus economy. It is a matter of sharpening children's eyes so that they don't carelessly overlook things, don't slip into a throwaway mentality but realize their value and begin to collect things. It is worth stirring our own minds to this too; what a lot of things can be done with old pots which might seem already to have departed this life!

Just as the first, almost unheeded coltsfoot by the wayside can be a real joy, so an empty margarine carton can inspire you to create attractive little baskets; Easter chickens can be formed from pads of cotton wool or little cradles from nutshells; all sorts of things can be manufactured.

The basic idea of drying is to conserve beauty, to grasp and keep memories. And the more perfectly you dry, the more fun

you have in creating an arrangement and the more pleasure you can give.

Go round the house and there are memories everywhere, happy and painful. Seeing the dark red Baccarat rose, you remember a once beloved friend; a gold wreath under a glass cloche was what your grandmother wore on her wedding day.

What fun it is too to amble round the woods, collecting natural objects, always discovering something new and returning home with a rich haul! It sharpens our senses towards the beauties of nature.

'Man cannot have a good time for a thousand days uninterruptedly,' said the Chinese sage Tseng Kuang, 'just as flowers cannot bloom for a hundred days.' Since we can now keep our flowers blooming for more than a hundred days, shall we perhaps have more than a thousand days' prosperity?

I hope so, and I wish the same to you!

Methods of Drying, Mounting and Assembling

Drying plant material

There are many ways of preserving plant material. Each has its pros and cons and there is really no one perfect method. The only way is to try out the different possibilities suggested here and experiment with them, for not every method is suitable for every plant. Flowers dried in silica gel, for example, are very brittle and delicate, so they are less appropriate for robust-looking arrangements.

Hanging up

This is a good method for all flowers, grasses, sprays and small fruits. Small posies already tied up, single blooms preferably already wired, bunches of grasses and so on can be held together with an elastic band and then hung up head downwards in a dark and warm but well-aired place. How long the drying process takes depends on the degree of humidity in the room; on average you can reckon about two weeks.

Loose spreading

Petals and whole flowers can be spread out and left to dry on special drying trays, on cake-grids or in flat baskets. The containers should be placed in a dry attic or any other dry, well-aired place. Drying never takes longer than a few days.

In the oven

Leaves, flowers or fruit can be laid on a baking sheet and dried in the kitchen oven. The temperature should not be over 60°C/140°F; the door should be open. Half an hour is often sufficient drying time. An ordinary oven is particularly convenient for this method.

In a vase

Place a bunch of fresh flowers in a vase. Add water to 10cm/4in up the stems or stalks. By the time the water has evaporated the flowers will be dry. This can take up to three weeks, during which time you can observe the drying process.

Fresh flowers can be dried in various ways, for example just in a vase with a little water.

Drying with silica gel

Silica gel comes in the form of a salt with fine crystals about 0.2 to 0.5mm/¹⁄₅₀in. in diameter. It quickly draws the moisture out of flowers. Gel is usually obtainable from a chemist or a good florist and is sold under various trade names.

Silica gel absorbs moisture until it is completely saturated. When it is quite dry, in other words active, it is an azure blue colour. According to its degree of saturation it fades to a greyish pink, until it is no longer absorbent. It must then be strewn on a baking sheet, put in an oven at 150°C/300°F and left to dry out for about an hour. It will then be effective again and can be re-used as often as you like. This considered, silica gel is a good buy, however expensive it may seem in the first instance.

Silica gel is not poisonous but should nevertheless be kept out of the reach of small children. Should any be swallowed by accident, follow it with a plentiful drink of water. It is a good idea to store the gel in an empty biscuit tin with a firm closure that will keep out atmospheric moisture. Obviously it should be kept well shut after being filled.

Flowers and leaves to be dried in gel should not be damp. Flowers caught when they are half-open are ideal. If a flower is somewhat limp, the stem should be considerably shortened, cutting it diagonally, and placed in hot water or water with an aspirin dissolved in it.

Spray varieties like marguerites and marigolds must of course be completely fresh; the flowers can later be taken individually from the gel. The biscuit tin should be filled to a depth of 1–2cm/½–¾in.

The flowers should now be carefully embedded in the gel as described in the step-by-step instructions opposite. A rose takes three or four days to dry, while delicate flowers like snowdrops, violets and primulas dry in one day. As soon as the petal-tips feel like parchment and rustle slightly when stroked with a fingertip then the flower is done. However, if the calyx still feels damp, then the process must be prolonged.

Flowers can become brittle when left in the gel too long. The best answer to this is to lay them out on a cake-rack and leave them for a day, after which they become manageable again. The more delicate the flower, the shorter the drying time.

The flowers are dry when their petal tips feel 'rustly'. The gel will have lost its blue colour and become greyish pink.

The colour of the dry flowers will have changed only very slightly. They will be very brittle, however, and should be lifted from the container with great care.

Silica gel can be used over and over again. It only needs drying out in the oven, preferably spread on a baking sheet. When it has become blue again it is once more ready for use.

1. The flowerheads should be cut off leaving 1–2cm/½–¾in of stem attached. A wire can be affixed to this later.

2. The flowerheads are carefully bedded into a biscuit tin filled to a depth of 1–2cm/½–¾in with gel, according to the height of the flowers.

3. The flowers should stand as upright as possible, their petals not touching. They should be about 1cm/½in apart.

4. Using a spoon, more gel is carefully poured over the flowers. Take care to fill all gaps thoroughly, even between petals.

5. When the flowers are all well covered, more gel may be poured directly from the packet, but slowly and carefully.

6. Finally, satisfy yourself that all gaps are completely full of gel. If not, spoon a little more in. Then put the lid on tightly.

Workspace and tools

Your workspace should be big enough to assemble all your materials and tools within reach. The table should be beside a window or use a good lamp.

Your tools should include a good knife for cutting plastic foam, scissors for shortening flower-stems, cutting away bad parts, trimming frills and crêpe flowers and so on, pliers for bending wire and, most important, pincers for nipping out fir-cone tips, also wires, glue, paints and a brush.

Wires should range from fine and very flexible green wire to stubwires and binding wire in various gauges. Wire from electric cables can be very useful. Besides these you need decorative wire in gold and silver and in different thicknesses.

As well as an all-purpose adhesive, you need a special polystyrene adhesive, and a hot glue gun is an ideal tool. The base of many arrangements is plastic foam, available in cones, balls and blocks that you can cut to shape. In addition, straw bases for hearts, wreaths and other shapes can be bought ready-made, but are not hard to do yourself.

Mounting flowers dried in silica gel

For this you need wires, pincers, nails of various sizes and a hot glue gun.

It is very easy to construct a wire stem. Wind a small wire spiral round a nail. Use the pincers to trim off the spike that is usually left protruding at the top. Remove the nail. Dab a spot of hot glue into the spiral and quickly push the stub end of the flower stalk into it before the glue hardens. The flower is now held securely.

Hot glue sticks rapidly and well, but it will stick your fingers too if you are not careful, and that can be extremely painful!

The real stem looks more decorative and natural. This can easily be dried in the conventional way, preferably by the hanging-upside-down method. You slip a wire spiral between the flower stalk and the stem and proceed as with a wire stem. (See fig. 7 opposite.)

The little wire spiral can be hidden with green or brown florist's binding tape to make the flower more perfect. Green leaves can be wired or stuck on in addition.

Flowers dried in gel are extremely fragile; if you handle them roughly you will soon find yourself with nothing but a handful of petals. Luckily this can be repaired with a little skill. Flower petals can be stuck together again with the glue gun; you can even give the flower a different shape.

The wired flowers are then stuck into a polystyrene cushion or a block of plastic florists' foam until needed. This way they are held up and cannot get squashed.

Choose a soft background filler for the composition of the different arrangements. Freshly cut box, fresh gypsophila, mosses and ferns are ideal. The breakable flowers would all too easily snap against stiff material. If there is no fresh, soft background material to hand, stiff plants can be left for a while in a damp cellar or out on a balcony, so that they become softer.

To avoid damaging the fragile flowers during arranging, it is a good idea to work methodically from front to back or from top to bottom. To insert extra flowers into an arrangement at the end is extremely difficult. With large arrangements it is more efficient to use wired flowers (see p.14) which can be bent in any direction. Ceramic rings topped up with water then filled with box, for example, can be the foundation for pretty arrangements with wired flowers.

Never giftwrap fresh and dried flowers together, or the dried flowers will take up moisture from the fresh ones.

1. Use a paintbrush to remove the remains of gel from the dried flower.

2. To make a wire stem, first twist a small spiral round a nail. Remove the nail.

3. Trim the short end off the spiral with wirecutters.

4. Put a drop of glue from the glue gun into the spiral.

5. Quickly push the stub of the flower-stem into the spiral.

6. When the glue sets, wire and flower are inseparable.

7. If you wish to give the flower a natural stem, shorten the wire to a few centimetres/an inch or less.

8. Push the wire up the dried plant stem and seal the join under the flowerhead with a drop of glue.

A ceramic ring (above left), a ceramic rose (above right) or a small ceramic basket are very suitable containers for dried flowers.

Wiring

For delicate flowers you need fine, flexible wire. To stick flowers into polystyrene or plastic foam you need a stronger stalk, so the end held with fine wire must be twisted together with a thicker wire. With more robust flowers the thicker wire can be used from the outset.

In all cases the wire is generally bent into the shape of a hairpin, but with one prong longer than the other. The wire is then pushed through the flower so that the hook nestles in the middle of it. With spruce, larch, fir and other cones the wire should be slipped as far as possible under the scales and the two ends twisted together. Special preparation is needed for shapes that offer no natural hold for the wire. Rosehips, for example, should first be impaled on toothpicks, while nutmegs need a groove cutting all round with a sharp knife so that the wire can lie in it.

Decorative wire

This fine gold or silver coiled wire must always be threaded on to another wire of corresponding colour and thickness. It is used mainly for trimming spices such as cloves, cinnamon sticks, nutmegs and star aniseed, but can also be twisted round sugar lumps or crystals.

Spraying

Single blooms or whole arrangements may be sprayed with glitter, clear lacquer or dye. They should be placed in a suitably large cardboard box open only at one side to stop the cloud of spray filling the whole room.

Fixing candles

A strong wire should be bent with pliers into a hairpin and the bent section heated over a flame. The hot wire can then be pushed easily into the end of the candle. Leave 4cm/1½in of wire sticking out to secure it on to your chosen base.

Artificial flowers

Artificial flowers may be created from seeds and kernels, dried pulses, crêpe paper, soft paper napkins and so on.

Bases for seed flowers can be cork discs ½cm/¼in thick, cut from old wine corks, or cardboard discs, or buttons. Bore two little holes in the disc, thread wire through them and twist it together on the underside. Now spread it with glue and stick your various pips and seeds on in the form of a flower. Tweezers are very useful here, and it is a great help to insert the wired disc into plastic foam to leave both hands free for the work.

For crêpe paper flowers, cut strips 8cm/3in wide from the roll and fold these concertina-wise. Cut the top of the folded piece into a curved petal shape, open it out, slightly stretching each petal, roll the strip into a flower, teasing out the single petals and secure the base by twisting it round with wire. The resulting flower can then be mounted on a hairpin wire like a real one.

If you wish to enhance your flower with sepals, cut these out of green crêpe paper in the same way as the petals and stick them firmly round the base. To hide the wire, wrap it with green, self-adhesive crêpe ribbon or guttering.

Paper napkins can be used very much as crêpe paper but `unfortunately cannot be stretched so the results look less lifelike.

Posies

Posies can be assembled in cone, dome or free shape. The chosen flowers and other material should first be laid out in a row in the order in which they are to be assembled. Short pieces should be wired first. Then small bundles are tied together and placed within reach.

If you have decided on a symmetrical form, choose a particularly beautiful flower as your central point and group the small bundles around it a row at a time. Everything must be securely wired in as you go so that nothing slips or becomes distorted. Each new row should be set slightly lower than the last to build up the desired rounded or conical shape.

Finally crêpe ribbon is wound round the bundle of wires and stalks. A paper frill and ribbons give the finishing touch.

Arrangements and baskets

Like posies, arrangements can be dome-shaped, conical or free. One determining factor is the container, its size and shape, material and style.

1. First pack the container with plastic foam, then stick in background material . . .

Another is the position where the arrangement is to be displayed. If it is to stand in a niche, it is enough to do a front-facing arrangement, but a couple of stones should be laid in the container as a counter-weight, so there is no chance that it will tip forwards.

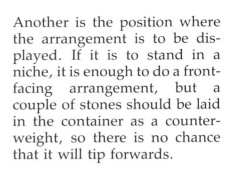

2. . . . for example box, until the base is completely covered.

3. Beautiful single blooms are distributed and introduced as focal points.

This is how the finished arrangement looks. Blue ribbon bows give it a festive look.

4. Piece by piece every gap in the arrangement is filled.

Wreaths, hearts and original shapes

Florists and craft shops stock basic shapes in straw, polystyrene or chicken-wire, but these can also be made at home. Most of them are only filled on one side so that you can have either a flat or a more raised shape. All the necessary material should be laid to hand, particularly small tufts already bunched. These bunches, together with single flowers, wired fruit and cones, are fixed onto the chosen base with wire, string, staples or pins. They should be added one to the left, one to the right, very close together, rather tighter in the centre and looser towards the edge. Baubles, candles or bows are not added until the end.

Balls, trees and cones

All three shapes use the same mechanics, a base of polystyrene or plastic florists' foam. Cones and balls in these materials can be bought in various sizes. The porous plastic florists' foam is easier to work on, however stems sit firmer in polystyrene.

In order to keep to the even curve of a ball or the shape of a cone, flowers and bunches should all be furnished with hairpin wires and set upright so that they all protrude to the same length. The base should be very closely covered. Balls can be given a decorative ribbon bow, which must be very well secured so that the ball can be hung up by it.

Trees also start with a ball base. If you need a very big ball, you will probably have to cut it yourself from plastic florists' foam by buying the biggest block available, rounding off all the corners and wrapping it in plastic or fine wire netting.

Mount this ball on a stick or branch, which must be anchored in your chosen container. For this you could try painting a plantpot. You then mix up some plaster of Paris, place the stick upright in the pot, fill it up with plaster and leave it to harden. The plaster can be masked with some suitable material like soil or moss.

1. Stick a plastic foam or polystyrene ball onto a suitable branch.

2. Begin to insert small bunches of material into the ball.

3. The finished tree is thickset with flowers.

16

Care of arrangements

Posies and arrangements made of flowers dried in silica gel are very sensitive, not suitable for a damp atmosphere or for out-of-doors decorations. They should not be subjected to strong sunlight either, or their delicate colours will fade. Dried flowers can be made more resistant to sunshine and will last longer if treated with hairspray or other lacquer.

Arrangements of conventionally dried flowers may be carefully dusted with a soft paintbrush and then sprayed with lacquer. This will strengthen them and give them a longer span of beauty and 'life'.

Dilapidated dried flower creations can also be sprayed with glitter, silver, gold or copper. This gives them an interesting gleam and they look as good as new. Although the original colours can never be restored, the 'new' arrangement will be more glamourous.

Dried posies are delicate, but can be treated
with hairspray or lacquer to be made more resistant.

Spring

The field and garden's lovely hours
Begin and end with thee.
For what's so sweet as peeping flowers
And bursting buds to see.

What time the dew's unsullied drops
In burnished gold distills
On crocus flowers with unclosing tops
And drooping daffodils.

A spring stroll

Grasses of different varieties can be mounted in plastic foam and then tinted with pink spray. Dainty lilac-pink immortelles, red and white tulips, parrot tulips and alpine violets enliven the arrangement. As a small reminder of the departed winter it can be softly decked with angel's hair. Sprays of mallow seedheads look particularly effective.

A spring basket in red, white and blue

A lot of delicate grasses and seedheads of various kinds are arranged in an olivewood basket. Among them are inserted royal blue irises, red and white tulips and red and white de Caen anemones.

Spring ducks

The first small primroses emerge from the ground, the hazel catkins, male and female, peep from bushes at the edge of woods and streams, the first daffodils and, of course, the forsythia blossoms delight us with their lovely intense yellow. All these flowers will dry excellently. When they are arranged in moss with ivy for a touch of green they will give us joy at least all through the spring. If you keep your eyes open you will find containers whose colours blend harmoniously with the flowers.

20

Palm Sunday

Palm fronds

With the blessing of palm fronds on Palm Sunday Eastertide is ushered in. Evergreen leaves are composed into a so-called 'palm bush', which may, however, include arbor-vital (thuja), box, holly, juniper, yew, fir (abres), larch, oak, pussy willow, hazel, ivy and other evergreens, all decked with coloured ribbons and in some regions apples and fancy bread too. The most important are of course the hazel catkins.

Many believe that the sacred greenery has the power to bring healing and prosperity. It is supposed to help against illness, for example, and protect fields from weeds. People also place some near the four corner-stones of their houses. In some places in Europe children go through the streets waving sticks hung with ribbons and red-painted eggs to drive winter away.

If you too are a little superstitious you can hang a palm bush outside your door to bring luck and a good harvest.

Easter

Full oft at early seasons mild and fair
March bids farewell with garlands in her hair
Of hazle, tassles, woodbine's hair sprout
And sloe and wild plum blossoms peeping out
In thickset knots of flowers preparing gay
For April's reign a mockery of May.

Easter wreath

Embellish an olive wreath with daffodils, sprigs of cherry blossom and an ivy trail. Hang blown and painted eggs from it by long ribbons and perch fluffy little chicks on it made of cotton-wool with red felt beaks.

Blue anemones

Rose-pink and moss-green hare's-tail grasses (lagurus), chive flowers, tiny white immortelles, quaking grass and vivid blue de Caen anemones are combined with a clutch of Easter eggs and a couple of homemade cottonwool chickens to make a fine Easter arrangement.

Easter baytree

A potted baytree placed in the hall will look lovely with an adornment of dyed and painted Easter eggs, with bright pink and yellow flowers stuck among its branches. Half-eggshells can be used as tiny baskets filled with moss and planted with primroses, snow-drops and cherry-blossom. At the foot of the tree grows a small meadow of cress and moss with clumps of snowdrops.

Hogweed umbels

Seedheads of hogweed or cow parsley can be found in any hedgerow or wayside. Gather with care as some of these plants can cause a painful rash. They can be adapted and used in many ways. Pink bows, cottonwool chicks and tiny pink baubles complete the arrange-ment. This is suitable as a table centre, with the advantage of being daintily sparse enough to see your fellow diners through.

Easter vine

An excursion in the countryside often brings lucky finds of material that lends itself to magical transformation, such as a old rooftile encrusted with moss and lichen, a fallen bird's nest dislodged by a storm, or a strange tree-fungus. Look out for knarled and twisted branches; the illustration shows an old vine stem which has been transformed into a decoration to last over Easter. Stuff a plastic florists' foam ball with box and preserve it with a spray of clear lacquer. Fresh colour is supplied by de Caen anemones and tulips with blown and red-dyed eggs mounted on small sticks. Cooked and coloured quail's eggs in a nest complete the composition.

Spring garden

About eight days before Easter sow some cress seeds on damp cottonwool, which must then be moistened daily. You can almost see the cress growing! Tuck half-eggshells, small prim-roses, tulips, irises and daffodils into it, add more eggs painted with natural colours, and your little Easter meadow is com-plete. It will last as long as you can resist the desire to eat the cress and eggs.

Daffodils and brown eggs

Colour harmony: brown hen's eggs, blown and spiked onto skewers, yellow and mauve primulas with their own leaves, roses, tulips and daffodils in different shades of yellow are arranged in fresh box.

Pink willow-wreath

Spray a small wreath of willow twigs in fasion pink. Add a posy of early violets, a couple of daisies, a parrot tulip and some pink-dyed eggs, and your Easter greeting is quickly made. This charming wreath can be adapted in a number of ways. The result is an easy-to-make gift you will want to keep.

Cheery Easter posy

This posy is cheerful and eye-catching with its bright colours on an original ground. Green parsley is interspersed with red roses, purple anemones, painted eggs and blue ribbons. The use of parsley is an imaginative touch which will make this posy very special. It could be a get-well gift.

Blackthorn wreath

Blackthorn can be found both in rural and urban areas. Wear leather gloves when bending the twigs — they are very thorny. Attractive brown hen's eggs, a couple of quail's eggs, small hazel twigs and some daffodils comprise this composition, which can be produced with very little expense.

Easter greetings

This arrangement makes a lovely little present to take if you are invited out at Easter. On a mushroom-shaped base, obtainable from craft shops, or in a low jug, you mount little tufts of evergreen box. Between them are blown eggs dyed or coloured blue and green mounted on skewers. A note of colour is provided by bright yellow tulips, small twigs of cherry blossom, pussy willows and a few snowdrops. A small cottonwool dicky-bird completes this colourful composition.

Easter tree

Take an attractively twisted branch or a piece of driftwood and use your glue gun to stick it onto a slab of tree-trunk as a base. The join can be disguised with a little moss. Hang prettily painted Easter eggs on the branch and make little baskets out of half-eggshells stuck on ribbon, filled with moss and set with snowdrops, coltsfoot or daisies. Those of you who are not very skilful painters could glue small petals, leaves and grasses on the eggs instead. Look for example at the deep pink egg with tiny blue flowers attached to it.

Easter basket

Sometimes when you buy soft fruit it comes in a little match-wood trug, and it seems a pity to throw it away or leave it lying about. It is admirably suited to an Easter decoration, filled with moss to support a few graceful grasses, two or three daffodils and a blue freesia.

Floral gems

Small, coloured yoghurt cartons too can be made into pretty table decorations, at other times of the year as well. Flowerheads are stuck round their rims and they hold half-eggshells decked with flowers and grasses.

Ladder Tree

In rural areas of Western Europe ancient Easter traditions are still observed. The three-rung ladder tree, the tree of life symbolizing the growing family, father, mother and child, seems quite a pagan one. And in fact the roots of Easter customs do lie partly in old Germanic religious beliefs, which were then mixed with the younger Christianity.

The evergreen bush is supposed to represent the Holy Ghost, while the Easter eggs symbolize Jesus' twelve disciples. The six-spoked wheel is the symbol for the birth of spring, the sunwheel, the sign of the ever-returning sun which endows the Earth with abundant growth and gives renewed strength to all.

To make the tree, a branch must be fixed upright on a slice of treetrunk. If you are lucky you may find one that already has three 'rungs', otherwise you will have to tie more branches on crosswise. The whole thing is then thickly covered in box. Fancy loaves form the points, dyed and painted eggs are hung on, and a few flowers are attached to announce the arrival of spring.

May

Come queen of months in company
With all thy merry minstrelsy.
The restless cuckoo absent long
And twittering swallows chimney
    song
And hedge row crickets notes that
    run
From every bank that fronts the sun
And swathy bees about the grass
That stop with every bloom they
    pass.

May basket

A ceramic basket is filled with moss. Moss cushions are always an ideal base for filling baskets and bowls decoratively. Many different kinds of beautiful moss can be found in woodland fringes, on old walls and dead trees. With the first lilies of the valley — the flower for May,

pink lilac, pink and white roses and white de Caen anemones stuck prettily into the moss, you can bring May into the house. The fresh and lively colours of the flowers of May are ideal to preserve. This means you can have spring-time in your home all year round.

Mother's Day

Yet summer's iles upon thee still
Wi nature's sweet unaltered will
And at thy birth's unworshipped
*   hours*
Fills her green lap wi swarms of
*   flowers*
To crown thee still as thou hast been
Of spring and summer months the
*   queen.*

Anemone bouquet

This arrangement is dominated by dark blue and white de Caen anemones. An iris, pink roses and snapdragons, quaking grass, eucalyptus leaves, a white tulip and gypsophila are added and a bow of pale blue ribbon completes it.

  You can even use quite a plain box for flower arrangements if you paint it beforehand. The container is important when planning an arrangement, so save boxes or containers of useful sizes. They can then be decorated when needed to suit the occasion.

Mother's Day ring of roses

Fresh red roses are wired onto a wire ring, very tightly because they will shrink a lot as they dry. Your mother will enjoy this wreath for a long time, first fresh and then in its dry state. The roses should be sprayed with clear lacquer. White roses dried in silica gel can later be inserted into any gaps.

Happy heart

Your Mother's Day greetings should be as cheerful as the colourful flowers on the box-covered heart. A wire shape is used as a base and sprigs of fresh box wired on thickly, then many wired flowers are inserted. Flowers of all kinds and colours may be used, roses, ranunculus, de Caen anemones, antirrhinums or crocuses. A few heart-shaped biscuits add the finishing touch.

Mother's Day heart

Make the heart by using green wire to fix moss onto a straw or wire heart-shape. The heart is then wound round with a long string of pearls and red, white and cream roses are tucked into it. To lighten the effect, tiny immortelles can be inserted between them.

Left: Happy heart
Right: Mother's Day heart

Whitsuntide

The trees still deepen in their bloom
Grass greens the meadow lands
And flowers with every morning
  come
As dropt by fairy hands.

White vase

Red roses and peonies are combined with delicate lilac-pink rhodanthe and little immortelles like edelweiss.

Coffee pot

A valuable antique coffee pot is decorated with Whitsuntide flowers. Irises, peonies and fruit-tree blossom make up this elegant arrangement.

Engagement and Weddings

Wedding Anniversaries

Traditionally, each anniversary is an occasion to celebrate. For all these anniversaries there are many ways to create something suitable and memorable with dried flowers.

 1st Paper
 2nd Cotton
 3rd Leather
 4th Fruit and Flowers
 5th Wood
 6th Sugar
 7th Wool
 8th Copper and Bronze
 9th Pottery
10th Tin
12th Silk and Fine Linen
15th Crystal
20th China
25th Silver
30th Pearl
35th Coral
40th Ruby
45th Sapphire
50th Gold
60th Diamond
70th Platinum

The young girls whisper things of love
And from the old dames hearing move
Oft making 'love knots' in the shade
Of blue green oat or wheaten blade
And trying simple charms and spells
That rural superstition tells,
They pull the little blossom threads

From out the knapweeds button heads
And put the husk with many a smile
In their white bosoms for awhile
Who if they guess aright the swain
That love's sweet fancys tries to gain
Tis said that ere it's lain an hour,
T'will blossom wi a second flower.

Myrtle wreath

In classical Greece myrtle was the symbol of youth and beauty, dedicated to the goddess Aphrodite. This origin is doubtless the reason why to this day brides have continued to wear a myrtle wreath as a distinctive decoration at their weddings.

Betrothal wreath

This wreath of red roses is for the head of an engaged girl or even a bride. Why should wedding flowers always be white, never red, the colour of love?

Wedding wreath

Sprigs of myrtle are twisted into a wreath with wire, preferably including a couple of flowering sprays. If it is the wrong season for myrtle blossom, gypsophila or cherry or apple blossom could be used instead. In some European countries the wreath may be preserved and framed.

Bridal bouquet of spices

In the old days a bride was sometimes given a posy of medicinal herbs. This custom was observed mainly by European peasant people in remote mountain valleys.

The posy was supposed to bring luck, signifying that the future household would never run short of the things included in it.

A further significance of the posy was that the bride should not enter the holy state of matrimony until she was able to name all the medicinal and culinary herbs and use them correctly. The background to this was a vital necessity. On solitary mountain farms it was important that a young woman should be skilled in medicine and be able, if the occasion arose, to deal successfully with sickness, death and the Devil.

People also wished the young bride wealth, so it was not merely for effect that silk flowers, pearl rings, satin and silk ribbons, silver and even gold ornaments were bound into the good-luck bouquet. With a little skill you can create such a posy yourself.

Wedding arrangements

White tulips, primulas, freesias and ranunculus are pushed into a little box-filled basket. Small sprigs of cherry blossom soften the effect.

A white mother-of-pearl bowl with white de Caen anemones, roses, parrot tulips and white ribbons make a symphony in white.

Wedding tree

Wire up a lot of little tufts of box and set them closely into a large ball of plastic florists' foam. The green ball is then decked with numerous white bows, white roses and white crêpe flowers. The stem is bound with white ribbon.

For the marriage

Fruit blossom, roses, tulips and white ribbons are set in a ball of box. This wedding tree will last for a long time to add floral beauty to the home.

Copper or Bronze wedding

A ball of plastic florists' foam stuck with box no longer dew-fresh is sprayed with copper-coloured paint. The decoration consists of a lot of sky-blue ribbons, white flowers and blue apples.

Rose wedding

Beautiful rose blooms are arranged in a large bunch of gypsophila. To perfect the illusion fill the vase with water. Incidentally, flowers will dry well even in slowly evaporating water.

Parsley wedding

It is hard to find an explanation for the name of this wedding anniversary, which in some Western European countries celebrates 12½ years of marriage (half of 25). Perhaps from now on you have to cook particularly well in order to keep your marriage going successfully!

Here roses are stuck into a bunch of parsley. The arrangement could be imaginatively adapted for some of the other anniversaries.

Silver wedding

Twenty-five years of marriage is marked with the silver wedding celebrations. A quarter of a century of marriage should be rewarded by those who are invited to the celebration. This ornate little wreath is made of silvered larch cones, small white apples, cloves bound with decorative wire, aniseed, cinnamon, statice, silver balls and poppy heads.

Golden wedding

Many different kinds of cones from our native conifers form the background for this wreath. All the fircones and beechnuts are gilded. Gold bows, baubles, pearls and all sorts of spice decorated with decorative wire richly ornament the wreath. With such a variety of material one must be careful to design an ordered and harmonious arrangement.

The same material can be used to decorate a little golden tree for the golden wedding couple, and the stem can be bound with broad gold ribbon.

Trees for the other wedding anniversaries can be made in similar fashion.

Baptism

Christening tree

A delicate creation of white silk roses, white immortelles, star anise and cloves bound with decorative wire and a white bow should embellish baby's naming day.

Little bunches of the different materials are made up then wired onto a stick and bent out into the form of a tree.

Christening heart

A christening gift that the god-mother or godfather could make. A plastic foam heart is stuck with statice, then pink-edged white roses, small white freesias, pink and white tulips and primulas are added. An iced pastry doll completes the arrangement.

Summer

Now summer is in flower and nature's hum
Is never silent round her sultry bloom
Insects as small as dust are never done
Wi' glittering dance and reeling in the sun
And green wood fly and blossom haunting bee
Are never weary of their melody.

Round field hedge now flowers in full glory twine
Large bindweed bells, wild hop, and streaked woodbine
That lift athirst their slender throated flowers
Agape for dew falls and for honey showers
These round each bush in sweet disorder run
And spread their wild hues to the sultry sun.

Rose basket

Summertime is rose time. To save a little of their scented glory for winter, dry some red and pink roses in silica gel and arrange them with fresh gypsophila to make an opulent bouquet.

A summer's day

Captured in a basket are all the colours and shapes of a summer's day in a flower garden. A Madonna lily, carnations, roses, fuchsias, pansies – all that the abundant garden affords – are arranged with grasses and small blue immortelles. The apple, the large cranberries and the mandarin are all preserved too. Roll them first in beaten eggwhite and then in powdered sugar. This makes an airtight seal and the fruit will keep for a long time.

Old Master

Delicate half-tones are combined with intense red and yellow, as in the faded paintings of old masters, to form the glorious abundance of an old-style still-life.

Red and blue

The dominant colours in this bunch are red and blue. Roses, pansies and larkspur combine with gypsophila, honesty and yarrow (achillea) to reflect the colours of the pottery jug.

Hay wreath

It is easy to make a delicate wreath of hay. Line a savarin ring or hollow-centred cake-tin with aluminium foil and press hay into it, spraying repeatedly with lacquer. In a very short time you will have made a pretty hay-wreath that can be finished however you like. The wreath here was decorated with lilac-pink rhodanthe, dainty quaking grass, and other little pink and orange flowers.

Hats in full bloom

Old European customs are being revived. One of these is the hatdance, which is being performed again at summer parties. An old straw hat is decorated with flowers and ribbons, put on top of a pole and held aloft. A loving couple tries to catch one of the ribbons. When they have, the ribbon then passes from couple to couple, and whoever is holding it when a bell is rung may keep the hat.

Florentine straw

Auntie's old Florentine straw hat celebrates its own Renaissance on the head of the youngest gardener. An old doll's summer hat too lay neglected for a long time.

Lady in a hat

A small plaster bust is trimmed with a cheerfully decorated hat. The summer straw lying beside it has its own blooms.

Birthdays

My wild field catalogue of flowers
Grows in my rhymes as thick as showers
Tedious and long as they may be
To some, they never weary me.
The wood and mead and field of grain
I could hunt oer and oer again.
And talk to every blossom wild

Fond as a parent to a child
And cull them in my childish joy
By swarms and swarms and never cloy
When their lank lengths oer morning pearls
Shrink from their lengths to little girls
And like the clock hand pointing one
Is turned and tells the morning gone.

Surprise trees for children

A tree like this is intended as a wonderful surprise and delight for children. A branch with attractive twigs, an apple branch for example, is plastered into a clay pot, weighted with stones and hung with various sweets. Of course the decoration can be made to suit any occasion: tiny parcels, crackers and gift-bags at Christmas, and chocolates, jellybabies and chewing gum for a birthday.

Birthday ring

Walnut shells are stuck onto a plastic foam ring and cinnamon sticks and little bows fitted into the gaps. A number of candles are mounted on the nutshells in accordance with the child's age. The centre of the ring can be filled with larch-cones and oak-apples. Pixies, which you can easily create yourself, join in the party. Empty drink cans imaginatively painted serve as place-markers. For older children you can stick a dried cherry branch in each can.

Owl tree

This is an unusual idea which gives children a lot of fun. On the twigs of a branch perch little owls. In a nest, which might be found on the ground in a wood after a storm, lie golden eggs. The owls' bodies are small larch-cones, their wings are made from the scales of fir-cones and their beaks from cut-off spruce-cones, then stuck on and painted red. Their eyes are the paper discs from a hole-puncher. The branch is put into a suitable ceramic container filled with plastic foam. This little tree makes an original decoration for a child's room.

Scented cone

A present for people who enjoy sweet smells, and also an unusual table decoration. A plastic foam cone is stuck with numerous roses, with cinnamon and cloves in between. A lemon rolled in stiffly beaten eggwhite and powdered sugar and stuck with cloves crowns the tip. Reed ribbons add the finishing touch. The scent can be renewed when necessary with oil of cloves or roses to give this appealing arrangement both colour and fragrance. The scented cone will enhance any room on any occasion.

Opal glass

A sweet-smelling bunch of freesias and immortelles is arranged in a glass vase.

Composition in yellow

Deep yellow chrysanthemums, primulas, roses and forsythia together with gypsophila make a picture which is harmonious in shape and colour.

Silver basket

Fresh and cheerful-coloured freesias, orange roses, daisies and green leaves are arranged together. The composition looks especially elegant and showy in the silver basket.

Victorian posy

Let us turn our attention to pastel-coloured roses, cornflowers, daisies and the delicate meadow chervil.

'Victorian' posies can be made from most summer flowers. They are particularly pretty either in very strong colours or in pastel shades. An important accessory to such a posy is the frill, either of paper or coloured lace.

Summer birthday

Everything that summer's generous bounty yields can find a place in a lavish birthday arrangement, with roses always being the essential ingredient. This colourful composition requires as simple a container as possible, like the white porcelain bowl shown here. As this arrangement will keep a long time it can be used to give summer birthday joy to people who are not lucky enough to have been born in summer. Whether for a summer or winter birthday, it will be treasured.

51

Colourful summer basket

Summer flowers of all kinds are arranged with statice in a basket and trimmed with ribbons.

Little basket

A willow basket is filled with box and pink gypsophila, to which are added moss roses and ribbons.

Pompom dahlia

In a crystal block are two delicate roses, a few grasses and a few green leaves with a dark red dahlia in the centre.

Tree in lilac and red

The base, as for most trees, is a ball of plastic florists' foam, or equally well a polystyrene one. The essence of this tree is its subtle lilac and red shades. Lilac-pink statice, dark red roses, delicate pastel-coloured acroclinium and white roses with red edges are bound together in small bunches, mounted on wire and pushed together into the ball. To tone with the mixture, pink and blue ribbons have been chosen. Moss and acroclinium cover the ground from which the tree springs.

Green plants

It is a nice idea to give friends who enjoy house plants a green plant combined with flowers of a different plant, in this case freesias.

Pastel blooms

Pastel-coloured ranunculus, de Caen anemones and roses bloom among grasses in an olivewood basket.

Birthday tree

A large ball of plastic florists' foam is secured to a pole that has been plastered into a large pot. The ball is first filled with statice, then honesty, various coloured roses, *Achillea* 'The Pearl' and yarrow, hare's-tail grasses (lagurus) and matt pink apples are artistically interspersed. With silk ribbons added and the plaster in the pot hidden with moss and stones, it makes a wonderful birthday present.

Reclining rose bouquet

Blue larkspur, asters and roses are arranged in a decorative bouquet that will give the recipient joy for a long time.

Nest of eggs

A hay wreath stuck with unsophisticated helichrysum and yarrow (achillea) and bound round with a pearl necklace is filled with lovely brown eggs from the market – or perhaps from your own hens. An amusing and original present for someone whose birthday is at Easter. Anyone particularly inspired could inscribe a quotation or motto on each egg for each year of age.

Rosetree

A standard rose, which breathes its last in winter, blooms anew. Small rosebuds and silk leaves are stuck on with a glue gun.

Perrier Jouët

It would be a great shame if a decorative champagne bottle, in this case handpainted with Emile Gallé motifs, were to land in the glass recycling bin. In keeping with the Art Nouveau ornament, white de Caen anemones can be arranged in it. If you present this together with a full bottle, you are sure to give pleasure.

57

Blue and yellow birthday tree

Palm branches, dune grass and helichrysum are the main material of this tree. Round the stem winds a piece of Traveller's joy (Clematis vitalba) found in a country hedgerow. According to your taste you can introduce roses and silk or other artificial flowers.

Two dark red roses

A charming composition of male hazel catkins, an iris and two red roses forms this small birthday greeting.

Wooden tub

Moss is stapled onto a ball and gaily trimmed with roses, statice and wine-red ribbons.

Festive trees

Little trees can be given to mark any occasion. Poppy seed heads or wild lilies, for example, can be suitably arranged on a ball of plastic florists' foam.

The arch

An arch makes a change from a container and can tone prettily with an old family portrait, a mirror, or even a flower picture. An ideal base is a wire coat-hanger. First, wind the hook with ribbon, then decorate the hanger from the outside towards the middle, keeping the two sides symmetrical. The middle can be filled with cones and larger flowers to give a balanced arrangement. The basic material of this arch is brown butcher's broom (ruscus), combined with red-painted larch-cones, blue-painted beechmast with pearl centres, gold, silver and pink baubles, cloves, star anise and cinnamon sticks trimmed with decorative wire, and dried roses.

Summer pot

A large bunch of statice is trimmed with roses, marigolds, larkspur and pansies.

Autumn and Harvest Thanksgiving

Autumnal mood

Leaves of various trees are sprayed with glitter and strewn artistically on a table. Sweet smelling honeycomb and sunflower seedheads are grouped about. A bee feeder serves as an original vase to hold a splash of yellow roses. Angel's hair lays a veil of gossamer over the picture.

Little autumn tree

Dried leaves and helichrysum are stuck onto a twig supported in an old teacaddy filled with gravel.

All haunt the thronged fields still to share
The harvest's lingering bounty there.
As yet no meddling boys resort
About the streets in idle sport.
The butterfly enjoys its hour
And flirts unchased from flower to flower
And humming bees that morning calls
From out the low hut's mortar walls
Which passing boy no more controls
Fly undisturbed about their holes.

Honesty tree

If allowed to grow unchecked, honesty and chinese lanterns would soon fill the entire garden. Stripped of leaves and seeds and dried, the combination of these two plants makes an enchanting impact. Sprays of honesty can be built into a tree with the help of adhesive tape and often a strengthening wire. It can be plastered into an empty tin can, the plaster hidden with white gravel. The delicacy and beauty of these plants make an arrangment you will never tire of.

Last roses

Grasses of all sorts are dipped into a bath of Easter-egg dye; others are sprayed with glitter. They are combined with roses, pompom dahlias and home-made artificial flowers.

Cress panicles

Watercress seedheads are trimmed with blue immortelles.

Hay harvest

Sweet-smelling wreaths can be woven from a sackful of hay. Bunch by bunch it is strung into a garland, then the ends are joined together. Delicate acrocliniums are tucked under the string, and among them fat helichrysums with their vivid colours. Red roses and bows complete this Harvest Festival wreath.

Bramble wreath

Hang an outdoor wreath on your front door in autumn. This one consists of bramble runners. It is easy to make if you wear thick gardening gloves. An interestingly twisted root, red ribbons, red roses and artificial apples decorate the wreath.

Mussel season

This wreath makes a jolly welcome for guests invited to a fish supper. Using a glue gun, empty mussel shells are stuck on a wire and then fastened onto a wreath of broom stems (juncus). Lemons must of course not be left out. They are stuck with cloves and fixed on with wire. Finally the wreath is wound with a toning ribbon.

Anniversaries

Nostalgic hanging basket

If you have any flowers left over from last year which were not perfectly stored and have lost some of their beauty, you can nevertheless make them into a charming composition. Slightly shapeless, with soft, gentle colouring, together they present a harmonious arrangement.

Miniature wreaths

You can give joy and express regards and good wishes on all sorts of occasions by creating tiny wreaths like these.

Cinnamon circlets

Break cinnamon sticks down the middle and glue them to a ring of plastic florists' foam. Add some cinnamon sticks

bound with decorative wire, star anise, flowers, and cloves with a pearl in place of a seed. Decorative wire makes a spider's web over the whole ring.

Lucky basket

Dahlias, marigolds, pompom dahlias and calceolarias are combined in a colourful bunch. Among them are some four-leafed clovers as lucky charms for the recipient. The basket is a different colour on each side.

Rosetree

Conventionally dried yellow and red roses are united on a ball with statice and yellow bows.

A generous bunch

To a generous bunch of fresh gypsophila are added dried roses, anemones and ranunculus. If you put a little water into the glass vase it gives the impression that they are all fresh flowers.

Winter

Basket of box

Evergreens belong to Christmas. Not many of them will keep for long but box and holly are two that will. A handwoven willow basket is filled with box. Gilded fragments of honesty and teasels are introduced. Snow-fairies of beechmast and felt hang among the leaves and glass hearts dangle on white ribbons.

Christmas is come and every hearth
Makes room to give him welcome
*   now.*
Een want will dry its tears in mirth
And crown him wi a holly bough
The tramping neath a winter's sky
Oer snow track paths and rimy
*   stiles*
The huswife sets her spinning bye
And bids him welcome wi her
*   smiles.*

Each house is swept the day before
And windows stuck wi evergreens.
The snow is beesomed from the door
And comfort crowns the cottage
*   scenes.*
Gilt holly wi its thorny pricks
And yew and box wi berrys small
These deck the unused candlesticks
And pictures hanging by the wall.

Hung wi the ivys veining bough
The ash trees round the cottage farm
Are often stript of branches now
The cotters christmas hearth to
*   warm*
He swings and twists his hazel band
And lops them off wi sharpened
*   hook*
And oft brings ivy in his hand
To decorate the chimney nook.

Blackthorn in winter

Wind a wreath of blackthorn and set it with Christmas roses, the symbol of life, being careful not to spear them like thorn-birds. Small ivy leaves add a touch of green.

Tree with pastry hearts

This tree is especially suitable as a winter gift. Stick fir cones into a ball of plastic florists' foam and fill the gaps with flowers made of seeds and spices. Pastry hearts hung on long red ribbons can be secured with wire onto the ball.

Wild lily wreath

A breath of foreign parts surrounds this wreath. The seedheads of wild lilies go with native fir cones and poppy heads to form an unconventional combination. This exotic winter arrangement can be used in many ways, with candles as an Advent wreath, hung up on the front door, or as a table decoration.

Wintertime

At this time of year fresh flowers are usually very expensive, so dried flowers come into their own as small presents and to embellish your home. Painted cones, waxed kumquats, hawthorn hips, poppyheads, wild lilies, pine cones and cotton capsules are bunched together with sprigs of box.

Christmas roses

Fill a small pot with fresh box and other evergreens. The pure white petals and yellow stamens of everlasting Christmas roses dried in silica gel lend a particular magic to the period leading up to Christmas.

Advent

Poppy wreath

This is a very special sort of wreath that can survive many pre-Christmas periods. Poppy heads are stuck thickly into a ring of plastic florists' foam with cinnamon and cloves in between and with blue bows and blue candles. Lastly the whole thing is wound round with a long string of pearls.

Santa Claus cone

Fill a plastic foam cone with fir, spruce and larch cones and decorate it with little Santa Claus figures and angels of beechmast and cones with papier mâché heads, red candles and cradles made of walnut shells.

Willow wreath

Evergreen holly, which keeps its shiny green leaves all winter, spruce cones, little red apples and green and gold Christmas ribbon decorate this wreath of willow stems.

Hogweed umbels

Hogweed seedheads can be found in any hedgerow or wayside. This arrangement makes a distinctive decoration with its pink baubles, pink bows and blue angels. These are easy to make yourself. Shiny blue foil is laid over a tin angel, pressed down and then cut out.

Wine-red wreath

Beechmast, fir cones, dried roses, dark red twisted candles, little apples and baubles appear in different tones of brown and red. A touch of glitter and a glass heart make this wreath a special Christmas pleasure.

Anemone wreath

If you are already longing for spring you can make your Advent wreath a little different. Pack a moss ring full of statice and trim it with small blue apples, azure bows and candles and, as an out-of-season surprise, blue de Caen anemones 'fresh' from silica gel.

Bauble trees

Little trees of fir cones, trimmed with baubles, apples and ribbon bows make suitable small 'thank you' gifts at Advent.

Advent candle-holders

A little candle-holder like one of these could be a cheerful and lasting gift for a lonely or old person. They are made from polystyrene, large fir cone scales, poppy heads, beechmast and all sorts of small cones. The point of interest is a flower dried in silica gel, either a rose or a Christmas rose. Or it could be a dried rose dipped in liquid wax or a kumquat preserved in the same way.

Christmas

Christmas cone

This cone made from nature's Christmas presents is a tree of a very special sort. Seedheads of various flowers, grasses, nuts, thistles, and even some seedheads of African flowers are stuck into mistletoe, box and holly. To keep everything completely natural, beeswax candles spread their honeysweet aroma.

The same every year

Every year the Christmas crib or nativity scene is set up. But this time there is a special addition, a willow basket bursting with Christmas roses.

A lovely rosetree

A plastic foam ball is thickly set with box. The trimmings are all red; roses, blown-glass hearts and a lot of shiny ribbons make the tree cheerful. It can be used at Christmas, or even for a rose wedding anniversary.

Happy Christmas To all

Little angels of beechmast dressed in white felt, white ribbons and bells trim this fir cone tree, together with half-walnutshells cradling tiny babies.

Glass bauble cone

This elegant and arresting composition can be either all silver and white or else red and gold.

Christmas cones

Cones are a very pretty substitute for large Christmas trees. Straw figures of angel musicians, pink apples and rings of wooden beads fit well into a beechmast cone.

Pearls, cinnamon, aniseed, cloves and nutmegs trimmed with gold decorative wire are the main ingredients of the aromatic spice cone. Fir cones, pink bows, pink baubles, cinnamon, pink apples and rings of pink-coloured wooden beads, trimmed with silver decorative wire create a one-tone cone.

St. Valentine's Day

Bishop Valentine lived and died over 1700 years ago under Emperor Claudius II. In spite of being forbidden to do so he married lovers and presented them with flowers. Thus he became the patron saint of lovers. The day of his death, 14 February 269, has become symbolic of love, sympathy and neighbourly charity. The pleasant custom of giving flowers to friends and people we love is probably connected with him.

Dainty wreath

A plastic foam ring is thickly set with pink and white statice and completed with red and white tulips and anemones, little red hearts, pink ribbon bows and quaking grass.

Loving greetings for St. Valentine's Day

Pink roses and blue and red anemones are arranged with fresh gypsophila. Gypsophila is ideal to use, because it adapts perfectly without disturbing the brittle blooms. Red hearts introduce a breath of romance. With roses you can often use their own stems and stick on dried leaves with the glue gun.

Right: Dainty wreath

Top: Loving greetings

Table decorations

Gorgeous flowers on a finely laid table

In winter we shouldn't deny ourselves colourful and gorgeous table decorations. All we need to do is dry our favourite lovely flowers in silica gel during the summer and then we can soon conjure up a decoration. Roses, pansies, larkspur and marguerites last very well. If you have glass tableware, try a pretty new idea of laying dried flowers and leaves between two plates. A summer theme for a dinner party during the dreary days of winter is a happy surprise for everyone. The beauty of dried flowers helps create a warm and lively atmosphere.

Doll decoration

Here is a splendidly exhuberant flower arrangement for a doll collector. Beautiful roses, marguerites and vetch are laid out with ferns and the dolls sit amongst it all. Not everyone is a collector but the idea of using items from a collection as table decoration is certainly a good one. Some people may collect paperweights, others unusual matchboxes, old tiles, antique tin toys or suchlike. A party table decked with flowers and collector's pieces lovingly arranged will always look inviting.

Menu card

In harmony with the ribbon, the card is decorated with a blue de Caen anemone and a bunch of snowdrops. Seasonal flowers are a good complement to an enjoyable meal. A beautifully decorated menu card will be taken home by guests as a momento of a memorable occasion, and may even be framed.

Advent stand

An old forgotten Advent wreath stand is dragged from its slumber and revived with scented rose-wreaths. Its tip is crowned with a clove ball. The roses and cloves emit a wonderful scent that envelops the table.

Cabbage tree

An amusing and uncommon table decoration for an autumn mealtime. A particularly fine root is stuck onto a slice of treetrunk and trimmed with a little moss. Onions, ginger, snailshells and garlic are grouped casually about it. The head is a Savoy or a red cabbage.

Potpourri

Sweet scents

A potpourri makes a very special present which can be put together especially and personally for each occasion and each friend. Pack a mixture of sweet-smelling leaves, herbs and petals in an original glass or a pretty sachet. The potpourri will release a heady fragrance as a long-lasting reminder of the giver.

Acknowledgements:

Photographs: Claus Arius, Taunusstein-Orlen
Front cover: Reed International Books Ltd/Constance Spry
and Cordon Bleu Group/Jan Baldwin

Poetry: Extracts from *The Shepherd's Calendar* by John Clare

First published in 1988 by
The Hamlyn Publishing Group Limited
This 1994 edition published by Chancellor Press
an imprint of Reed Consumer Books Limited
Michelin House, 81 Fulham Road, London SW3 6RB
and Auckland, Melbourne, Singapore and Toronto

ISBN 1-85152-557-2

Produced by Mandarin Offset
Printed and Bound in China